# A Book of Peace

## Messages to Inspire and Nurture Peace

### DAWN KATAR

**BALBOA.**
PRESS
A DIVISION OF HAY HOUSE

Balboa Press books may be ordered through booksellers or by contacting:

Balboa Press
A Division of Hay House
1663 Liberty Drive
Bloomington, IN 47403
www.balboapress.com
1-(877) 407-4847

ISBN: 978-1-4525-4854-8 (e)
ISBN: 978-1-4525-4853-1 (sc)
ISBN: 978-1-4525-4855-5 (hc)

Library of Congress Control Number: 2012904233

Printed in the United States of America

Balboa Press rev. date: 10/02/2012

For my beloved Twin Flame

# Foreword

Like many, I have busy days, stressful times, and family worries. Sometimes, days would go by without giving 'peace' a thought. Out of the blue, with the world rioting and a myriad of threats abounding, "Point of Peace Messages" began appearing every night in my inbox. Over the course of a month, it became quite apparent that these little messages recalibrated and centered me each evening.

Soon, the smart phone was overloaded with "saved" peace messages. Some of the messages became meditations; others were practical, often in a humorous mode. All were inspirational. All were truth.

The little book you hold in your hands may be one of the most important tools of this age. Unlike a novel, you may choose to read this book from the back, middle, or by centering yourself and opening it as a personal daily message. However the book is used, there is a key power in each message.

Much has been written about the power of 'intent', whether it be in the form of prayer, meditation, or positivity. Let the messages flow into your bones, your cells, and your soul. From afar, I see the world reading these pages: anger and fear dissipate, while the points of light become brighter.

I am humbled by the invitation to write the Foreward for a book with so much wisdom and truth. I also must thank Katie Dawn for her daily commitment to this important work. As more people become accountable to be centered and peaceful, our world will certainly reveal itself as the Garden Planet it always was meant to be.

Suzanne Powell, MSN, MBA

# Preface

It was many years ago that I was guided to begin using a mantra/ affirmation in most of my in-between times. I was to repeat it one hundred times. This translated to waking up time and before bedtime. I was soon reminded that the process of saying this simple prayer required only one or two minutes and that while I was at a traffic light or in line at the grocery store, it would be appropriate to use this tool. I began to feel great and in a better frame of mind on my job and at home (and of course, in traffic). I noticed that my patience level in uncomfortable moments was growing and strengthening. This simple mantra is "I am peace."

In 2011 my soul called me to begin sending a daily message by e-mail to anyone who wanted it. Attuning to the frequencies of the Divine, I would type out a few sentences that were presented to me by various Archangels and Ascended Masters. After several months, many of the recipients asked that I put these messages into book form, as they were finding them so valuable every day and they didn't want to let them go astray in their e-mailboxes.

I have been blessed with a gift of Spirit to hear and receive these transmissions of Peace from the highest realms of Light. It is my joy to share this gift with you and I trust that your personal peace will expand whenever you read and apply the teaching they offer.

I recommend that you pause for a moment after reading each message to have a deep breath and mentally decree, "I AM Peace." That simple statement can be in your breath throughout the day and you will begin to notice that Peace is your natural state of being.

In gratitude and with blessings,
Dawn Katar
1/21/12

*B*eloved Ones, do you know that the feeling of peace, tranquility, and calm is available to your experience no matter what the outer world tells you—no matter what your chattering mind tells you. I invite you to breathe deeply, letting each breath go forth as a quiet statement to your world that you let go of all the chatter. Each breath brings you deeper to the reality of calm, to your inner sea of tranquility, to true Peace. Practice this often. Namaste.

*Ascended Lady Master Nada*

*P*eace is not the absence of conflict. Peace is the presence of Love which is All That Is. Be filled with Peace. Be filled with Love. In this state of consciousness, there is simply no power in perceived conflict. Namaste.

*Cosmic Buddha*

*D*o you know peace? You have met before, but perhaps you do not recognize it when you have it so close. Once you have found peace, you must seek it again and again. Be still. Be slow. Be aware. You will recognize it within you. It is easier to find when you seek it often. It becomes a close friend who will stay closer and closer each time you seek it. You will always answer, yes, I know peace.

*Ascended Master Tsen Tsing of the Council*

ome have called me the Queen of Peace. You may call upon me to assist you in quickening your natural state of peace. I will be with you whenever you call for me. In Love, I AM your

*Mother Mary*

*T*he startling thing about this world is that humans think so little of Peace that you can bear it for only moments before you seek to contradict that experience with discomfort and unfaithful behaviors. It seems humans are waiting for the Messiah to show up again and again to take away the discomfort and bring peace. How long will this world wait for someone to do this for them? How many times will humans demand they be saved and refuse responsibility? The world has been given the tools and the knowledge to live in peace by many Truth-bringers. Why do you still wait?

*Ascended Master El Morya*

*S*halom. I bring you peace. My beloved ones, today your peace is assured as you dwell in the house of Love. Where I AM, thou art. I AM Peace. Thou art Peace

*Jeshua ben Joseph*

*I*f you want to know peace on earth, invite it to your dinner table. Tell your family that for this time you will not say anything cruel or angry. For this time you will smile and be pleasant to one another. This is not the time to go on and on about the troubles of the day, but a time to let that all go and to let peace sit with the family at your table. Your food will nourish your body, mind and soul. Your attitude will nourish your family and the planet. After dinner, bring the peace into your other living space and share about the joys and troubles of your day. Lift one another up and let peace bring you deeper into your hearts.

*Ascended Lady Master Ariana, Goddess of Truth*

*T*here you see unrest and discord in your community, you have a human responsibility to bring forth your peace and bless it all. If everyone who can see this need would stand for peace and step out of the confusion of the world at large, soon that world would shrink in the presence of peace and would become the world at small. Then, Peace will be the world at large where it is easier and easier for individuals and communities to resonate in that new world.

*Ascended Master Saint Germain*

*O*nly Peace begets Peace. One cannot force peace by controlling the outbursts of fear and its companion anger. Learning to respond to what appears as negativity to your ego and mass consciousness with a deep breath of relaxation and prayerful blessing will have lasting effect. If the world does not respond to your Peace instantly do not be fooled. Peace, which is an element of Love, cannot be withheld.

*Jeshua ben Joseph*

**W**hat if Peace was never more than a breath away? Why would you doubt that? Be assured that when you practice Peace, you have a quiet humor about you. You get the joke of the universe—All is Love. All is Peace. The rest is a lie you once believed.

*Cosmic Buddha*

*O*nce you have read this, close your eyes and relax your body and your breath. Then send Peace to all parts of your physical body. Say to each part, "Be at Peace. I Love You." You will feel exquisite.

*Ascended Lady Master Ariana, Goddess of Truth*

*S*tart with a relaxing posture and begin reciting "I am Peace" on each in-breath. Count them to 100. If you use this as a filler of your time while waiting for other life moments (like when on hold on the telephone, or in line at the supermarket, etc.) you will cultivate a habit that serves you and humanity. What else are you doing with your thoughts in those moments? (That is rhetorical, ha ha!)

*Ascended Master Tsen Tsing of the Council*

W hat can you express today that will sponsor Peace in your world? Are you contributing to Peace?

*Mother Mary, Queen of Peace*

*D*o you believe as the foolish do that if guns and war ceased to blare there would be world peace? It would be wondrous indeed for the outer violence to cease. But the stillness that leaves is the place that peace can be heard and become expressed. Still your personal blaring of anger so that peace can be heard within. Then the outer world will sense it also. The world says "Shhh . . . Did you hear that . . . I thought I heard something soft and sweet . . . Be still so we can hear it." Ahhh. Peace.

*Ascended Master Saint Germain*

*I*s there anything peaceful in your work day? Look for it and celebrate it! Do not be deceived that others control your peace. Only you can determine your life.

*Joseph, the Caretaker/Father of Jeshua*

**W**ho have you known in this life that has felt like a tormentor to you? Fill yourself with Light and Peace and imagine that one now enveloped in this Light and Peace. Forgive that one and yourself with the freshness of peace. God in me forgives all. Amen.

*Ascended Lady Master Nada*

*A*llow us to summarize these powerful messages: Peace is a certainty. Move beyond hope that you will know peace in your time. Allow yourself to commit your fullness of Being to experience it as every breath. We extend all Love to you as you dis-create the false shapes of all that you have believed stands between you and your True Nature of Peace.

*Jarusha, Light Bearer of the Golden Age*

*D*uring these challenging moments in human history we remind you that you have all been through it before and have survived, and resiliently thrived. Your soul knows that whatever the world chooses, you have it in you to dance in the Light and bring Love to it all. So, if you might feel the tension or tightness recall this Truth. Nothing can keep you from Peace except as you forget who you are. Always come back to the thought, "Ah, I remember. I'm alright. I bring the Light. Peace is my Path."

*Ascended Master Tsen Tsing of the Council*

*I*magine that you are sitting in a perfect spot in a spring meadow. The birds are happily singing and the breezes flow through the trees. You are peacefully alive in the vibrancy of life. The scent of flowers fills your breath and the tickling of the grass plays with your hands as they skim their soft blades. In this meadow the peace of belonging allows each of the unique features to have a place here, as nothing interferes, All harmonizes to one experience of bliss. Such can be your every experience in every place. Allow each feature of your experience to be a perfect gift and rejoice as one feature blends with another. Breathe in the Peace of each expression and rejoice that you have created it to be Here.

*Ascended Lady Master Nada*

*W*hen you are clear in your intention for Peace, amazing things occur in your life. Sometimes, you are blessed with an old pattern of non-peaceful reactions so that you can bless the experience and declare Peace where once you might not have. Other times, you find yourself experiencing simplicity through life moment where it is a joy to declare your gratitude for the Peace. In all ways, Peace comes to you to choose. Be clear in your intention for Peace so that your holy self can celebrate your mastery of choice. Each experience is an initiation to the highest frequencies bringing you closer and closer to One with your I AM Presence.

*Ascended Master El Morya*

B e not afraid of what you do not understand. Seek to know that Love is in all—manifest and un-manifest. Therefore, you can embrace what you do not understand in order to know Love. Be at Peace, my brethren, and let your Divine nature be the compass. Understanding is not the Key to the Kingdom. Love, which is in all, shall open all doors to wisdom, joy and peace.

*Jeshua ben Joseph*

*Yield now and be at peace with Him, thereby good will come to you.*

*New American Standard Bible, Job 22:21*

*T*o yield, to surrender, to let go—these are some of the most challenging phrases for the human ego to hear. Yet, we say to you, the most peace you can know comes when you allow yourself to surrender to the Highest. And in that Peace, you truly have all grand and wondrous energies and manifest come forward.

*Jeshua ben Joseph*

*T*he world is a peaceful place.

This is a peaceful planet.

You are (I am) a peaceful individual.

Everything in your (my) reality reflects peace.

Say these kind of affirmative statements frequently, especially when you might be tempted to believe the illusion of non-peace. It is a simple shifting technique.

*Mother Mary, Queen of Peace*

*W*ould you let peace flow through you if your life depended on it? Well, it does, my friend. And how can you let peace flow though you? Each in-breath fills you with Spirit (inspire). Each out-breath let's Spirit express (expire). When you focus on your breath, you prime your pump and the Peace flows. If you notice some thought or emotion that wants to deny Peace, put in into the breath and it will transform itself into the Spirit of Peace. Try it . . . . Your life depends on it.

*Ascended Lady Master Ariana, Goddess of Truth*

Your untamed ego may say to you, "If that person would just be still and go away, I could have some peace." Say to your untamed ego, "Be still and go within, and you will find peace." Tame the ego so that it will be the partner on earth that your soul values.

*Ascended Master Serapis Bey*

*W*e share here an important message regarding how some view the history of creation with regards to the "fall" of Angels and Humans from Divine. Please use your breath, your heart and your mind to call Peace to all perceived history—battles between good and evil, Michael and Lucifer, and so on. Do not dwell in this interpretation any longer as it perpetuates an inevitable unending war within. All of this is a "story" and is not real. We have brought forward some of these interpretations in your past so that you could use the story as a basis for understanding your spiritual evolution. Let us now dis-integrate the false wars and re-integrate the Peace of a loving, all inclusive God/Goddess/All That Is. What if you have always been Free? What if there was nothing to fear? What if every battle could be mended into the Love of All?

*Archangel Michael*

*P*eace is calm. Peace is passionate.
Peace is smooth. Peace is dimensional.
Peace is pensive. Peace is animated.
Peace is deep within. Peace is expanded without.
Peace is a choice. Always. All ways.

*Cosmic Buddha*

*I*f Peace is not with you today, you have forgotten something of great importance. When the outer circumstances of your life tell you that Peace will come later, if at all, then you must have a deep cleansing breath and you must decree to your world "Whether I see it or not, Peace is here. Whether I feel it or not Peace is here. Whether I hear it or not Peace is here. Whether I think I know it or not, Peace is here." Have another deep relaxing breath and settle into the Truth. Let go of the lie.

*Ascended Master Saint Germain*

*W*hen do you choose to forgive a thing? Once you have run through all of the available emotional energy? When someone has begged or been humbled sufficiently for you ego satisfaction? The quicker you recognize that you are holding a judgment about someone or something, you have the power to choose to give it forth—to forgive. In this exercise, beloved masters, you experience peace.

*Ascended Master Tsen Tsing of the Council*

*T*here is always activity that you feel "must" be completed within a frame of time as you understand time to exist. Even as this may seem true for you, you can participate in the activity as though you have chosen the blueprint for your agenda and as though you have infinite time to enjoy the activity. This is not to encourage procrastination. Rather, to encourage complete involvement with the activity. Joy is now activated within and Peace flows as well. Your God self only wants the outcome of your Joy and Peace.

*Seth, an Evolved Collective Consciousness*

"**W**hy are there so many battles in the outer world?"

"Why can't humans learn to let love guide all relationships?"

These kinds of questions are asked by every remembering soul and the answers are best given as new questions. "Why is it that now is the moment for peace to express everywhere?"

"Isn't it wondrous that humans are remembering to let love guide all relationships? Thoughts and questions pouring forth expect to be answered with the same energy they have created. So, more of the same continues. Isn't it perfect that we get to create all the Peace imaginable by asking the better questions?

*Archangel Metatron*

B eloved Ones, do you not remember that I have said, "My Peace I give to you"? Do not refuse my gift. Be in stillness and receive it. I shall forever be with you in Peace. Let us rejoice that there is more to be received from our Father/Mother God than can be imagined on earth. Alleluia!

*Jeshua ben Joseph*

*W*here is the Love? It is everywhere. There is no place Love does not exist. Knowing this to be so, allowing this to be so in your life carries Peace on your breath. What better "place" to observe the illusions of the mass consciousness. As the observer, experiencing Peace Love, you have clarity, empowered choice and, most importantly—great humor!

*Ascended Lady Master Ariana, Goddess of Truth*

*D*o your best to reframe everything you hear as a message of Peace. This is a challenge in a world perceived as selfish, angry and downright mean. Yet, we say to you, there is a possibility of Peace in every statement. Even an "evil" intention cannot stop you from finding Peace. This could be your most fun game! So I will test you with an easy statement overheard from a High Spirited Soul in New Jersey:

"Do you want a Peace of me?" Go ahead . . . . laugh loudly and bring joy to the world.

*Ascended Master Saint Germain*

*O*ne of the simplest paths to Peace is forgiveness. Since forgiveness is the act of "giving forth" there is always something to give. As you forgive whatever you are experiencing, i.e. give forth completely to the All, you will feel the bliss of Peace move through you. That is the transformation of your experience into even grander Divine experience. Why not make forgiveness a daily ritual of Love?

*Ascended Master Tsen Tsing of the Council*

*G*entle breezes; gusty winds.
Each demonstration supports Peace.
Babbling brook; roaring river.
Each demonstration supports Peace.
Sleeping baby, tantrum-ing toddler.
Each demonstration supports Peace.
Imagine each of these demonstrations and feel the Peace that is possible.

*Ascended Lady Master Nada*

*I*f you haven't made Peace with physical death, now is a good time to recall that all form is temporary and all serves in Divine Order. Be clear about what is incomplete in your life and make Peace with such matters. Let all that is ready for the next step in Life be blessed and allowed to move forward. Today, live in Peace and rest in Peace. (P.S. Don't take this entire message SO seriously!)

*Ascended Master El Morya*

*I*t is a day for you declare Peace with all beloved ones sent to share with you on your path. They all desire that you Love them for who they are. As you desire to be loved for who you are. Much of the time, humans think they are seeking to be loved for who they think they are. You can receive and give love with the personality, but it seldom brings perfect Peace, since it is the illusion of the self which is doing the seeking.

*Ascended Master Saint Germain*

*L*et us have an imaginary moment where you visualize yourself having an encounter with a world leader of government. Experience yourself as your expanded God-Self and have a brief conversation with this person. Your message will only be one to four sentences. You will wait for the response and give one more sentence. How does it feel to bring Peace to your world?

*Mother Mary, Queen of Peace*

*T*here cannot be a world at Peace without your Peace. When you desire Peace within your body, your family, your work and home you will contribute the focus of your blessing on these arenas. It does little to wish for Peace without the willingness to bring it forth.

*Ascended Master Tsen Tsing of the Council*

*B*rothers and Sisters of Light, hear us. All the Universe is prepared to proclaim Peace on your planet. Sufficient of you must live the Peace and there will be such a quickening that even non-believers will be shifted by the wave that comes over all. Be responsible to your God-Presence and so it shall be. With all Love,

*Kalishar, Commander of the Ship of Love*

*W*e are all family. Sometimes you let the illusion of differences get in the way of accepting and loving. Even in your birth family, there are sometimes strains to think you are from the same source. Do not doubt that you can be raised by wolves in the forest and still be from the One Source. It matters not from whose loins you have sprung. Love one another without expecting sameness to prove anything. As a matter of fact, if you could look in the mirror and love yourself it only proves that what I have said is true. All one family.

*Ascended Master Lord Lanto*

*W*here are you going in such a hurry? What will occur if you allow yourself to cease running through your days. Slow your pace and slow your breath. Observe. Be aware. Live in a habit of full awareness and you will always be in Peace.

*Cosmic Buddha*

*E*ach drop of water contains the particles of potential ocean. Within each drop of water is the substance from which you came in earth and in heaven. The water you have sweat from your form, which flows through your veins has mingled with the waters of the ocean. The rain drops which dance upon your skin have been in your food and in your form. Do you realize how connected you are to all of life? It might bring you Peace to know that you cannot be separate from one another, from earth or sky or ocean. The water of Spirit connects all.

*Your Brother, Chief White Eagle*

**P** – E – A – C – E.
Powerful – Energy – Alignment – Causing –
Enlightenment. Thank me. You're welcome.

*Ascended Master Saint Germain*

*L*et the Light of your Being shine upon all in your world. It will illuminate the shadows and bring the possibility of Peace to the places which had been in hiding. When you choose to shine your Light, your personal shadows bring forth greater possibility as well. Embrace what the Light shows you and bless all so that Peace flows everywhere.

*Ascended Lady Master Quan Yin*

*T*here can be no other answer. Let go of your fear and allow the radiance of Love to express throughout your body. It is time for Father/Mother God to fulfill the promise of Peace through you. Peace is the result of allowing Love to fully express in you, as you.

*Ascended Lady Master Ariana, Goddess of Truth*

*W*hy do you weep, precious one? Do you not remember that I Am your brother and your friend? I know what it is to grieve the changes that may come. In my humanity I wept for the changes I saw in future time. Yet I have shown you that the I Am remains when the world is always changing. Let the Peace I Am cleanse you through the tears and affirm your Truth. All illusion shall pass away. Love I Am remains.

*Jeshua ben Joseph*

We are telling you that Peace in the world around you cannot persist if you believe it is a product of human power over anything. Such presumption leads to only more war or violence in order to enforce "peace". In the human experience of the satisfaction of winning, peace cannot persist. Enjoy the moments of a "win" and become still in order to experience the source of all Peace—lasting Peace.

*Kalishar, Commander of the Ship of Love*

*C*reate a sacred place in your home that reflects the most peace and joy imaginable. It might be a corner of a room or a full room dedicated to this sanctuary. It might be an object or cloth that you carry with you to make this space wherever you go. Place in this space the colors and images you most respond to as Peace. If you need to place a curtain of luxurious silk or gauze or brocade to mark the entrance do so. For some of you, this is not new information. For some there is a waiting for the right money or style and so forth to accomplish this small task. I ask that you let go of all excuses to make this space just for you. It will hold all the possibilities of Peace to support you in letting go of stress and limited thought. Imagine it in your mind and then allow the creation of it to unfold into your perfect manifest experience. Gifts of Peace will flow. Namaste.

*Ascended Lady Master Nada*

*T*here is a sacred code which translates to perfect peace and it is written within the Light of each of your Merkabah. It cannot be removed and it cannot be re-written. It is forever the Plan of Divine that it shall be available to all in any moment. The more you access this code, the more you seal the route of its expression—from the Source to your Three-Fold Flame and to everything you call forth from this sacred point of creation. When this code is realized to you, there will be an attraction to all Beings of Light that have realized the code as well. You are so close to the Infinite Peace that is this planet's destiny. You are so close to full manifest of your Light Body. The Light Body is not a vehicle of escape from chaos, but a vehicle of penetration through chaos into Creation.

*Archangel Metatron*

*W*hen you feel troubled within your emotional body do not resist the feeling. The truth you may realize with this is: Your emotions and feelings are not the same thing. Breathe deeply with the feelings within the emotional experience and allow yourself to become free of the attachment to the emotional response. The feeling will open up to greater love and Peace once you recognize that you and the feelings you experience are not the emotion that is programmed to express. Contemplate this.

*Archangel Gabriel*

R ejoice that the Mother of your worlds continues to birth anew. Rejoice that all worlds of creation continue to celebrate your world as a distinct, unique and wondrous place of arising consciousness. Only here can you realize that the cycles of life and death, of duality have purpose to bring you to Source of All. Love it all. Surrender it all. The sacred is the pulse of life I have given you.

*Gaia, Mother Earth*

*L*etting go of attachments brings Peace. Surrender your expectations for life to be a certain way, for people to respond in a certain way, for the "big payoff" for all you've done . . . Decree with your awareness of Source "I now let go of all. I surrender all. I am One in Spirit." How much Peace can you handle? How much Freedom can you handle? I dare you to do this daily and you will find out. Enjoy watching your strings of attachment fall away, fly away like balloons let go from a child's hand.

*Ascended Master Tsen Tsing of the Council*

*A*re you ready for peace? Perhaps not if you think you can no longer laugh or cry or even shout. Sometimes your belief is that peace excludes expression. Beloved ones, Peace includes all aware expression of you! Peace is you fulfilling your Divine expression without judgment, without fear, yet with acknowledgment of your connection with All.

*Ascended Lady Master Ariana, Goddess of Truth*

*T*uning in to Peace is as simple as answering your cell phone. Have a deep breath or two and say, "Hello. Here I AM." Peace will respond. Trust this.

*Archangel Michael*

*L*et me reassure you, beloved ones, that my Peace, your Peace is present. Please forgive the circumstance that interrupts this Truth. Allow Peace to be.

*Jeshua ben Joseph*

*W*isdom of elders tells us that we must be at peace with nature. Respect nature and learn from her. When you do not receive her gifts and thank her, you will fail to feel the joy that she has placed in you. Be at peace with nature and do not fear her. She has everything for you.

*Chief White Eagle*

*O*nce in a while, someone will come along in your life that brings an upsurge of joy to you just by being near you. Can you say that you are that someone for another? You cannot control another's experience, yet you can choose to smile and flow love from your heart. When that someone who has brought you joy comes close, be grateful to them and to yourself. Choose to beam your love and know that there will be another experiencing that upsurge when you come into their presence, even if you don't know who that is. Peace follows the joy!

*Ascended Lady Master Nada*

*O*ne simple prayer will give you the experience of Heaven on Earth. With the deepest relaxing breath say, "I AM Peace." No need to beg for it. No need to bargain for it. Just breathe and softly decree. And so it is.

*Ascended Lady Master Quan Yin*

*T*oday is the perfect day to remember that you can pack peace in your pocket, your purse, your suitcase to have handy wherever you go. When your daily travels feel stressful, just pull that peace package out and hold it to your heart. It cannot be confiscated at any checkpoint of your life. Don't believe anyone has the power to take it away from you.

*Archangel Uriel*

*T*here is more than enough Peace in this Divine Universe for every human to be filled up and overflowing with it. All you need do to claim your part of it is to open your arms, open your heart and allow it to flow. You do not need to earn it. It is yours.

*Ascended Master Paul the Venetian*

*W*hy is it that your natural state of Peace flows like the softest "Om" through your mind? Perhaps because you are "wired" to be inspired by certain sounds, certain sights to put you into the state of Peace. A baby sleeping, a mother's hum of a lullaby, a field of wildflowers swaying in a breeze . . . Why is that your natural state of Peace is available wherever you place your attention-intention?

*Ascended Master Tsen Tsing of the Council*

*B*eloved Friends, I have an analogy for you to consider. Do you know that when you look in your side mirrors on your vehicle you are told, "Objects are closer than they appear"? This is your life process. When you have set an intention in prayer for your life experience, you are often looking for it to show up from every human angle. Trust that things are not what they appear from your human angle. Everything you need, everything you desire is closer than you can even imagine. You can realize Peace as you let go of watching for your good to show up from behind or alongside of you. Remember that "Peace is closer than it appears". Namaste.

*Ascended Master Saint Germain*

*P*eace is the natural rhythm of the Universe. This is a monumental Truth. Peace is a reality that allows all creation to be as it is. We ask that you serve the possibility of Peace for All.

*Elohim, Servers of the Divine*

*W*ill you have peaceful thoughts today? Interject a peaceful thought to your chattering mind every few minutes. "Today I am having peaceful thoughts." Try this when your mind is its busiest. This kind of interjection of new thought is the perfect "monkey wrench" to dismantle the old machinery of human thought. At the very least to your experience, you can have a chuckle at the notion that such a simple act as this can shift your entire day's experience!

*Ascended Master El Morya*

*L*et Peace fly. Let it soar. Let Peace land on a blade of grass. Let it light upon your nose. Let Peace lift you up and land you in the midst of life. Renewed. Refreshed. Let Peace.

*The Heavenly Cherubim*

*W*ould it bring you Peace to know that the Light in the tunnel of darkness is not a train heading for you? Could you surrender the belief that the Light is outside of you? What you see in the tunnel is the mirror of your Being. The closer you get to it, the brighter the reflection. Tah-dah! Enjoy the Peace of remembering that the darkness is the illusion.

*Ascended Master Saint Germain*

*L*ike shimmering moonlight, Peace falls upon the entire Earth. Perhaps because of clouds or the illusion of horizons lost to orbit, the shimmering moonlight seems unavailable. Yet, you know that the moon is still in her perfect place and the earth plays the game of "hide-and-seek". When you do not feel the presence of Peace in your part of the world, remember that you are playing a game and that it is always there. Smile, my children. Smile.

*Gaia, Mother Earth*

Y ou can know the truth about Peace starting from within, yet still look to the outer world as proof that is not yet time for our Era of Peace. Beloveds, accept your Peace within <u>now</u> and it will expand beyond you. You have no control over how others or when others will witness Peace. That does not change the Truth that it exists for all, right here, right now.

*Cosmic Buddha*

*W*hen Peace flows thorough you like liquid Light you are a much blessed ambassador to your world. When you feel you are parched and that Peace is a far off oasis, the world cannot see you, but can only see the shadow. Remember this; there is no shadow without Light. Please do not block the flow of your Peace, your Light. You desire that your world be in Peace with you. Do not live in the shadows anymore.

*Ascended Master Kuthumi*

*P*icture this: Every world leader is gathered in a great room where the walls are circular and not square. Each is facing toward the center of this circle and is bowing to the others in the room. There is nowhere to hide, nowhere to gather an army. The walls of this great room are crystal and reflect the colors of each of the leaders. The reflection is like the great aurora of all time. This is a beginning of World Peace. Thank you for bringing this vision to your heart.

*Mother Mary, Queen of Peace*

*W*hy can you feel Peace when no one is around you, yet the sound of another's footstep disturbs your Peace? Beloved Master, because you can be aware of many things occurring in your moment of experience does not need to be interpreted as lack of Peace. Use your awareness as expansion of Peace rather than elimination of it. You can choose this perspective.

*Cosmic Buddha*

*P*eace be with you. Always. All ways. Give your fears to me that I might bless them. Then let yourself be welcome with the Father. Shalom.

*Jeshua ben Joseph*

*W*hatever you think about your place in the world is what the Universe honors. I highly suggest that you think well of your life by blessing all aspects with gratitude. Behold Peace in your life. The Universe is not judgmental about what you think. It honors everything. Don't you want the Universe to see you and your place in the world as Peaceful, Loving, and Joyful? That is all up to you.

*Ascended Master Hillarion*

*L*augh out loud! Peace is a path with many giggles and grins. With only your ability to smile you can create the Peace you seek in your life and in the world.

*Ascended Master Tsen Tsing of the Council*

*L*ook into your heart to expand your forgiveness. Forgive everyone for everything. Peace beyond anything you can imagine will flow through you.

*Mother Mary, Queen of Peace*

eminder: Peace is not the absence of what you don't like. It is the complete acceptance of everything as an expression of All That Is.

*Ascended Lady Master Nada*

*L*ook deep within your heart and connect with your Three-Fold Flame. From this place of awareness, expand the Light to fill your body and your mind. Use this connection with your sacred I AM source to decree Peace to circumstances and expressions in your world. You must become familiar with this energy and allow it to launch all your thoughts and desires into the world. Peace is at cause for all good outcomes.

*Ascended Master El Morya*

*I*s your physical body at Peace with itself? Are you at Peace with your physical body? Most always symptoms of discomfort in your body are an opportunity for you to be more grateful for the process of all your physical systems that are working harmoniously for your good. The gratitude can bring more ease, more Peace to all of your bodies.

*Ascended Master Tsen Tsing of the Council*

*W*ithin every seed there is a Point of Peace. It is the space that created the seed to form. It is the space that creates the seed to grow. Whether the seed reaches full maturity does not measure the amount of Peace that is present for the seed. Remember this when you feel that something in your manifest world does not seem to mature to the ripeness, the destiny you have imagined. There is full Peace within it all.

*Gaia, Mother Earth*

*L*ove knows Peace. They are inseparable. If you are not feeling Peace, look for Love. If you are not feeling Love, look for Peace. Of course, if you are not feeling either, get very very still. Breathe. They will both show up and you will feel wonderful!

*Ascended Master Djwal Khul*

*A*rrange your day so that you have several appointments with Peace. Schedule these appointments so that you will honor and show up for. Peace will always be there to meet you. So, just as you would be prepared to meet with a client or your boss, or a date with a new friend, be prepared to meet with Peace. You know what to do.

*Ascended Master Saint Germain*

*D*o you feel Peace in every breath? It is often a matter of practice. When it is important enough to you, you will practice receiving peace. Practice calling it into your breath. So simple.

*Ascended Lady Master Ariana, Goddess of Truth*

B eloved Ones, may you know the fullness of Love this day and be with me in Peace. Where will you go this day to bring Peace to another? I know that the Father/Mother God desires that you bring your Peace to the world. It is the Loving thing to do.

*Jeshua ben Joseph*

*O*nce you understand the true power you have when centered in Peace, there is nothing that you cannot move nor shift with clear intention and breath. Your deepest Peace opens all possibilities.

*Cosmic Buddha*

*L*istening for the whispers of God is challenging while you are listening to the sound of leaf blowers and hedge trimmers, but it is not impossible. In fact, the more you practice being in Peace, there is nowhere, no earthly sounds that can keep you from hearing those sweet whispers of Spirit.

*Archangel Michael*

*W*hat does World Peace look like? If you choose to visualize World Peace do you start with the picture of how is seems to be now and then just eliminate the parts that you do not want to include? That is a confusing message to your Spirit. First, hold the vision of something small that represents Peace for you. Then expand that vision to include more and more of your world. That will be a most clear message for your Spirit and the World. Always include, rather than exclude.

*Archangel Uriel*

B y your very nature you are assured that Peace is yours to claim. Give it life with your proclamation. "Let there be Peace." And so it is. Just as you are taught that in the beginning it was declared "Let there be Light." And so it is.

*Archangel Metatron*

*W*ars are fought to find Peace. Isn't that silly? What if Peace was just allowed to Be? Wars could not continue. When your inner war is roaring nothing can be won. Allow Peace and your conflicts are resolved. When you begin to sense that you are about to become engaged in an internal struggle, have a deep breath and settle into the silence of Peace. Someone may ask you, "How have you figured out that problem?" Your answer: "God's got it."

*Ascended Master Saint Germain*

*R*emember to be aware of the Peace in Nature. Do not be fooled by high winds or storms, by certain species "fighting" over a meal. There is harmony in everything around you and Peace flows throughout Nature. Draw from this awareness and recognize you are part of this harmonious flow. You are Peace.

*Gaia, Mother Earth*

*O*ur Father, who art in heaven, hallowed be Thy name. Thy kingdom come. Thy will be done on earth as it is in heaven. Let Peace be ours this day. Let all receive the glory of the heaven this day.

*Jeshua ben Joseph*

*I* Am open for Peace this day.
I Am a perfect channel of Divine Peace.
I Am Peace.

*Archangel Michael*

*W*e love it when you sigh a Peaceful sigh, or giggle in the presence of Peace. We wish to assure you that there is no one appropriate response to the recognition of Peace. As you cultivate your abilities to experience it most often, you will find that each moment that you recognize that you live in the presence of Peace, you will notice that it brings you a smile, a sigh, a giggle, and even an uproarious laugh.

*Ascended Master Saint Germain*

*L*ike flowers glistening with raindrops in the garden Peace sparkles in your daily experiences, making the seeming ordinary come more fully alive. Peace makes everything more radiant. Another way to find Peace is to explore your experience with the joyous expectancy of abundant life. Do you notice the connection?

*Ascended Lady Master Nada*

*P*eace is not the reward for martyrdom. Examine your personal syndrome for martyrdom. There are aspects in most human's lives. Suffering for the sake of values is not a wise choice. When one chooses to live by values that direct the soul's journey on Earth, it is wise to do so in joy and in Peace. Leave suffering to other times and places that are now complete. Choosing Peace is its own reward.

*Ascended Master Sanat Kumara*

*L*ive. Recognize that you may have been experiencing your life as a journey of survival. When you claim your life as fully connected and expanding consciousness, you then experience yourself being alive! You allow yourself to use awareness as a vehicle of enjoying every breath and all that it brings. Most of all, you experience Peace because you do not doubt your Oneness with Source.

*Ascended Master Kuthumi*

*B*eloved Ones, it has been said, "March to a different drummer." I say, "March softly to the beat of your heart." Get to know your own heartbeat and your own rhythm of your Divine connection. This kind of march is steady and soft. It carries Peace in every beat. Shalom.

*Jeshua ben Joseph*

*W*hy do you think humans have created it to feel so difficult to Love one another? Could it be that they are afraid of Love? Could it be that without remembering that they are not separate from Love they feel competitive for it? How can one feel Peace when one is in a constant scramble to feel Loved? It is beyond important that each soul "do the work" of remembering Love is constant. Peace, therefore, is constant.

*Ascended Master El Morya*

*A* Peaceful Planet. That is what this planet was once called. Many long for the return of Peace. Peace has not gone away; it has been hidden by anger and fear. The choices each human makes to express love or fear either remove the false barrier or build it up. Every choice counts. Bless your fears and choose to express love. Peace will be seen in you and all around you. Everyone benefits as you allow your planet to be in Peace.

*Ascended Master Tsen Tsing of the Council*

*H*ail, beloved ones, full of grace. Allow me to assist with your Peace Process. Call upon my maternal bounty to wrap you in Peace and remind you of your connection with our Father/ Mother God.

*Mother Mary, Queen of Peace*

*L*earning to live as Peace is a gentle process of reminding yourself to stay detached from expected expressions and outcomes. Be curious and aware. Acknowledge all in your moments to be aspecting the Divine.

*Ascended Master Djwhal Khul*

Say unto your Master, "Yes, Lord, I will follow." You shall be blessed with Peace for you become the Master following each step. You shall know Peace as you will always be in the protective blanket of the Master's Love.

*Ascended Master Serapis Bey*

*W*ith all the activity of Light on and around the planet, do not mistake the increase in frequencies to be a challenge to remain in Peace. Indeed as you will choose Peace it will be more full and encompassing of your life than ever before.

*Ascended Master Sanat Kumara*

*A*h, Beloved Masters, we greet you with great joy this day. Do you know how I spell Peace? **P**erfect **E**nlightenment **A**s **C**hoice **E**xperience. Yes, it is all choice.

*Ascended Master Tsen Tsing*

*P*lease open your heart to one another. Do not be afraid. With your compassionate heart, you will share Peace with the world. What can you fear from the heart of another? Even the Grinch grows a loving heart in the presence of Love and compassion.

*Ascended Lady Master Quan Yin*

*I* Am that I Am. As you celebrate freedom from tyranny, allow yourself to feel the Peace of letting go of tyrannical thinking that has kept you in bondage. Let go of the past and the fears that your life might not change quickly enough. Truth is this: your life will change very quickly. It is the transmutation and transformation your Soul is seeking. Namaste.

*Ascended Master Saint Germain*

inning the lottery is not your ticket to Peace in your life. Those kinds of blessings are surely an opportunity to explore new ways of being in Peace. However, sometimes you postpone your Peace until the circumstances in your life change. Allow Peace now and let the miracles flow!

*Ascended Master Godfrey*

Someone recently asked me, "How often should I pray for Peace?" My answer is this. It is not necessary to ask God for Peace. It is necessary to use your prayer many times in your day to bring Peace through you. Pray prayers of Gratitude. As it is written in the Christian Bible, "Pray without ceasing"

*Ascended Master Tsen Tsing of the Council*

**W**ithout a doubt you are each participating in the Earth's most magnificent era of Peace. More and more humans are aligning with this desire and are creating more moments to enjoy the gift of Peace. As your brothers and sisters awaken to this possibility in their lives, the energy of Peace expands and the true "explosion" of this power will be witnessed by all. Do not let yourself indulge in thoughts of discouragement. Trust in Love.

*The Council of Shambala*

*T*he lesson of Peace is short. Heal every angry reaction you have. Forgive. Bless. Allow.

*Ascended Lady Master Ariana,*
*Goddess of Truth*

*L*ittle by little you are finding that you are the one that created the false world of dis-harmony. And with each realization that you bless, you are building the creation of Peace in your life.

*Chef White Eagle*

B eloved Masters, I wish to quote for you a wonderful idea presented by Jiminy Cricket. "When you wish upon a star makes no difference who you are. When you wish upon a star your dreams come true." You see, the universe does not discriminate. Wish for Peace. Wish for Love. Then go about your life as if it is true. Because it is.

*Ascended Master Tsen Tsing of the Council*

*B*ringing Heaven on Earth is a simple task. Peace exists as energy of Heaven. Heaven is here. Sometimes, we feel the urge to say to you, "Duh!" But that might sound disrespectful and impatient . . . So we won't say that . . . You are all such Grand Masters, and indeed you are all my Beloveds!

*Ascended Master Saint Germain*

*C*ount 10 things you are grateful for that you have not acknowledged in a while, or maybe ever. Now, for each thing you are grateful for say, "I bless you with Peace." This practice can bring your Inner Peace to great fulfillment. Your awareness of Peace increases each time you bless something or someone with the intention of Peace.

*Ascended Master Djwal Kuhl*

*O*f all the moments you have lived today, how many would you say you were conscious of being in a state of Peace? Review the day and insert Peace wherever you have forgotten to acknowledge its presence. You have so much more than you are even aware.

*Ascended Master Saint Germain*

*L*ife is not just a series of breaths, but life without
awareness of each breath is more empty than
full. Breathe Peace in each breath.
Walk in Peace, step by step.
In this awareness, your life will be overflowing beyond
full.

*Grandfather Lao Tsu*

*W*hatever you choose to do with the time which you count to make your life fit in your 3-D world it is wise to include plenty of meditation while believing that you have all the time possible in your world. This kind of faith will sustain you when you experience time to be shrinking or disappearing. Peace is worth every moment of your time as you know time to exist

*Seth, an Evolved Collective Consciousness*

*T*he forest is full of mystery. Most people look at the mass of trees and do not venture into the mystery of the woodland. As you look at your life as a forest, full of diversity and habitat to many living things, you will recognize that you are usually comfortable looking at the edges of your reality. The depth of the forest holds great Peace. Venture in toward the deepest part of your life and make Peace with all that dwells within.

*Gaia, Mother Earth*

*W*isdom of Love says that Peace is your choice. Wisdom says choosing Peace is the only real option. When you do not experience Peace, listen within for the voice of Wisdom. You will remember to choose Peace.

*Chief White Eagle*

*T*hink upon this Truth. All That Is cannot separate, judge or cease to Be. Your illusion of separation is made up of nearly countless beliefs which anchor your 3-D reality. The more you attune to One the swifter you experience the dissolving these false beliefs and the swifter you experience the frequencies of your 5-D actualization. This process requires that you suspend all you think of as "real" and dwell in the Peace of your true nature.

*Ascended Master Kuthumi*

*P*eace becomes you. Truly. Your face, your posture and your every movement wears Peace well. You look MARVELOUS, my Peace friend!

*Ascended Master Darius, Tailor of Athens*

*O*f all the possible places in your world that you could ever visit, there is one that is recommended more often than any other. Since before time and space became noted in your creation, the most wondrous "place" to enjoy has been your inner-most consciousness. It is referred to by great teachers by many names. Your secret temple offers more thrills and fulfillment, more Peace and Love than any earthly resort or destination. Best of all, it doesn't cost anything but your commitment to open your inner senses. Enjoy now. Thank me later.

*Archangel Jarael*

*L*et us look upon your beauteous countenance and rejoice that you are full of Peace. Your radiance reveals that you are fully blessed by the Light of God within. Create joy for your world with this acknowledgment that you are an instrument for Peace.

*Seraphim, Hosts of the Throne*

**W**hatever you do, do it with Peace. Whatever you say, say it with Peace. Wherever you go, bring Peace. If you intend this, the consciousness will lead your actions.

*Ascended Master El Morya*

*L*et yourself learn to communicate with Peaceful words, Peaceful expressions. When you observe someone with a Peaceful countenance, put into your mind that you will speak like that and act like that. Declare to yourself, "I will bring Peace into my world like this." There is no more effort to speak Peace, smile Peace and act Peace than to do so in discord. Let your smile guide your communication with the world.

*Ascended Lady Master Nada*

*I*f stars fall from the heavens, if earth wobbles and throws forth her inner core, let Peace rule your place in this Universe as it rules throughout all Creation. Put your fear into the Violet Flame of Transmutation and allow the Golden Elixir of Divine Immortality to run through your being. Peace shall rule in this sacred place.

*Ascended Master Saint Germain*

*W*ithin my heart there is Peace. Within my body there is Peace. Within my mind there is Peace. Within my soul there is Peace. Within my home there is Peace. Within my work there is Peace. Within my government there is Peace. Within my world there is Peace.

*Grandfather Lao Tsu*

*D*o you fret over the circumstances of your world governments? Sometimes you think you will be at Peace when the fighting and controlling stops. You have an arrangement in your thought process to hold to beliefs of uncertainty as an excuse for staying out of Peace. Perhaps you also hold to beliefs of confusion caused by those around you. If only "they" would come to agreement, your world would be less chaotic and more Peaceful. This may be true, but you (your limited ego) is the cause and You (your True Self) can choose to unravel the false beliefs and choose Peace NOW.

*Ascended Master Saint Germain*

*W*hen you have a desire to get to know someone more intimately, you invite them to share time with you, share a meal with you . . . maybe even share the night with you. You invest yourself. You are interested to know if this person can offer you something, add something to your life. Get to know Peace the same way. Invest yourself and be curious about your relationship with Peace. If you wish to start in small increments of your time do so. Soon you will want to share every waking and sleeping moment with Peace.

*Ascended Lady Master Quan Yin*

**W**orking in the world of day-to-day commerce sometimes may seem like drudgery or that it keeps you from your Spiritual focus. What if you affirmed Peace in your workplace? What if you allowed your workplace to be a place that people are drawn to because if vibrates as Peace? This is your choice.

*Ascended Master Tsen Tsing of the Council*

**B**eloved, there is nothing on this earth that can keep you from the Era of Peace, except the limited frames of your beliefs and unwillingness to be in your Heart with the Divine. You must know at this moment that what is promised is given. Go to your Sacred Heart and welcome yourself "home".

*Jeshua ben Joseph*

*L*ittle is remembered in your history of the Peaceful days on this planet. Though indeed there have been great cycles of Peace, be thrilled to know that you are participating in the shaping of this world's greatest expression of Peace. More humans are calling themselves to live as Peace and this has great effect upon this world. Do not stop your journey inward. Continue to bring forth your Peace and gift it to one another.

*Ascended Lady Master Empress Sylvia of Lemuria*

S ome people are still clinging to a belief and a hope that death will bring them Peace. While it is true that if one is awakened to Divine, you will have a welcoming Peace when you exit the physical body. Yet, as one is dragging their physical life down and is angrily waiting for it all to be over, Peace may not be recognized when the form is shed. Therefore, awaken now. Practice Peace now. Whatever your timing may be to shed this physical life do not wait for Peace.

*Ascended Master Djwal Kuhl*

*I*t is a wise one who stretches the physical body regularly. It is a wise one who stretches their understanding and belief patterns to broader and broader perceptions of their life. When one has a flexible body and a flexible mind, the soul is Peaceful, for it does not live in painful limitations.

*Ascended Lady Master Quan Yin*

*L*o, I AM with you always. My Peace is your Peace. All you need do is breathe your Heart Open and there I AM. If you will be with me now, we shall touch everyone with this Peace.

*Jeshua ben Joseph*

*W*ake up! Do you not hear the chimes ringing? Tis the dawning of a new age. All you need do is awaken and feel the frequencies within you and all around you. Then, rise up to celebrate and let go the shackles of old thought and restraint. Celebrate that you now choose to wake up the whole world. Wake up! Company's coming and we want you to be ready. We bid you Peace.

*Archangel Gabriel*

*D*uring this perfect moment there is Peace between the particles of your thoughts. If you slow your thoughts, you will notice the greater and greater flow of Peace. You can have Peace within your thoughts yet the denser the particles of your thoughts the "narrower" is the flow. Simply breathe and watch the thoughts lighten and the Peace flow widen. Interesting meditation, eh?

*Archangel Metatron*

When you hear news of things to come, choose to breathe in the Peace of letting go. Let go of needing to understand. Let go of needing to plan and control. Why run your mind through the obstacle course of confusion? Let go into Peace.

*Ascended Master El Morya*

*H*ow can you ever say you hate something or someone? Why would you say that? It is only that you forget the power of the words you speak and that you do not think you are worthy of Peace in those moments. Let yourself bless your speech and bless that which you curse with those words and thoughts. Then re-claim Peace as forgiveness opens up the energy and speak words of kindness brining Peace forward to your world.

*Ascended Master Tsen Tsing of the Council*

*B*eloved Ones, praying for Peace with the fear that humans are beyond hope and helpless to produce Peace is worth little in the immediate. All serves and so it will bring the lesson of Oneness with our Father/Mother God and the fear will be transmuted and integrated into the great realization: Ahhhhhhhhh—I am the one who must claim Peace, for it is always with me.

*Jeshua ben Joseph*

*I*m joyful to remind you to call forth Peaceful passage on all highways and travel systems for yourself and all who travel with you. So, when you are driving and someone seems not to notice you and attempts to drive their vehicle into your lane of flow—let yourself be in the habit of smiling and having a deep breath to smooth the transition. When the traffic patterns are slow and slower, smile and have a deep breath to smooth the flow and create a joyful wave of Peace. I tell you, from a third dimensional point of view, the heavens are teeming with Light Bodies and Vehicles, yet there is never a crash—only joyful encounters.

*Ascended Master Prince Olimat*
*(aka Saint Christopher)*

W ithin your life you experience many versions of your world. It varies by your mood or your focus. It would seem obvious then, that if you focus on Peace and choose your mood as Peaceful, such would be one of the most pleasant versions of your world.

*Ascended Master Serapis Bey*

We see Peace where you see pain. We bless Peace while you curse pain. You are invited to bless what you see as pain so that curses are lifted. What is cursed by you is what you shun and believe to be bad and wish to be separated from. What is blessed by you is what you welcome and believe to be as an opportunity to expand your Love and Peace. When you bless everything, your vision of life is shifted. Alleluia!

*Archangel Zadkiel*

*H*ail Beloved Ones. Gather near to me so that I may hold you in my arms and softly sing our own song of Peace. Let yourself feel rocked gently to the sounds of heaven that I bring to you. Let yourself feel your heartbeat merge with the song and let me remind you of the "place" that is home.

*Mother Mary, Queen of Peace*

*W*hen the world shows the old pattern of fear, rejoice that there is an energy seeking to be reformed. The old pattern of fear can give way to excitement and can be guided to new ideas and expressions. When one confronts the fears without judgment there is little room for the fear to continue to produce the control it thinks is important. Keep Peace within your vision for all outcomes. And remember, Pease is not the absence of discord, but the frequency of allowance and Love which cannot be stopped.

*Ascended Master Saint Germain*

*P*eaceful elections everywhere! You can hold that thought best when you don't try to also hold judgments about any of the parties on the ballot. Who now has more forgiveness and blessing homework to do? Hmmm . . . I thought so. We love you all, no matter what.

*Ascended Master Saint Germain*

*W*hen you awaken from this dream called your physical life, you will realize that you have had everything that could be desired within you all the while. The price you are paying to learn this is bigger than you know. When you journey within to where Source resides as you, the Peace that is there will override all else. This is reality. You become Peace. Peace becomes you.

*Ascended Master Kuthumi*

*A*h, beloved Masters, it is our joy to bring you this reminder. When you let yourself be at Peace with your physical body you accelerate the frequencies of your Ascension process. Do not look for Ascension as an escape from the physical. Rather, look at the physical as a gift to bring you to Ascension. Peace with your body means you do not judge the looks, the aging, or the chemical imbalances. You lovingly observe and bless. That is opening for Peace.

*Ascended Master Tsen Tsing of the Council*

*W*ith all that one sees and hears in your world regarding unhappy, angry people, it may be easy to believe that it is inevitable that it will spill into your personal life. Bless those events and choices being made and forgive yourself for any possible angry feelings you are holding onto. Make Peace within your emotional body and the world will find it easier to be in Peace.

*Grandfather Lao Tsu*

*T*oday is a perfect day of Peace. Have you been noticing? Start now and notice all the Peace that is flowing in and around you. I am there, blowing gentle Peace all around you. Breathe it in and enjoy.

*Ascended Lady Master Quan Yin*

*L*et us sing this day. Peace is our song. Create your verse and we will all sing the chorus. "Peace is ours now. Peace is for all. Peace is the gift of letting go. I let go. I let go. I let go."

*Archangel Jophiel*

*E*nergy in motion tends to stay in motion. Your intention for Peace, acknowledged frequently, is what builds the necessary momentum. Let the momentum of your energy expansion in Peace carry itself forward, upward and all around those who need the reminder of this most natural state of Being. In gratitude, we remain your friend in all Divine.

*Ascended Master Saint Germain*

**W**hatever you are feeling, our desire is that you acknowledge it and include Peace. There is always room for Peace without pushing away or negating all of your feelings. Most humans have mastered chewing gum and walking at the same time, so we have no doubt that you can be the Master of bringing Peace into all experiences.

*Ascended Master Hillarion*

*B*ring me the color of Peace. Shall there be only one color for Peace? Each of you will bring me a new color of Peace. For in your very breath you have a unique and glorious color of Peace. Beyond the rainbow's spectrum, your colors shimmer in the cosmos. See Peace in every color, in every expression.

*Ascended Master Lord Lanto*

*I* bring you the Peace that passes all understanding. It is sublime. It is graceful. You are living in that now. To access this Peace, open the shutters on your windows. Remove the covering from your eyes. See fully with your heart.

*Jeshua ben Joseph*

*M*ake Peace with your family on Earth. Forgive it all. Bless it all. Let go of it all. You have choices about your involvement and interactions and we encourage you to make Peace. No expectations and no strings. Simply allow Peace to flow in you.

*Ascended Master Tsen Tsing of the Council*

S tart accepting that you can know Peace NOW. The only thing between you without full Peace and experiencing full Peace is your mental/ emotional program that believes Peace must demonstrate by the outside "reality". We are indeed most joyful that you would choose this as an opportunity to place this program into the Violet Flame for transmutation.

*Ascended Master Saint Germain*

**W**ondrous Spirits, we are happy to share this reminder about Peace:

**P**erceive **E**verything **A**s **C**lear **E**nergy. Let go of the blame of other's misperceived circumstances, and you shall be in the perfect flow of Peace.

*Ascended Lady Master Ariana, Goddess of Truth*

*W*ith turmoil in your weather patterns and environ—mental issues, can't you smell the Peace rushing in? I'm not trying to be funny here, although I sense humor in your reaction to this query. Mother Nature may express with gusto, but Peace is always in her gifts. Please meditate upon this Truth.

*Ascended Master Brother Theodore*

*T*hink of the most tranquil place that you have ever visited, whether in the physical or in your mind. Now let yourself go to that place in your mind and feel the breeze; experience the scents and sounds. Feel the Peace. You can go there anytime. It is with you. Like most visualization exercises, the more you visit with full consciousness, the more likely will be your manifestation of this Heart's Desire.

*Ascended Master Djwal Khul*

*I*magine that for every hateful thought there was 10x more Love. Forgive every hateful thought that you created and sent forth. Forgive every hateful thought that you accepted was part of your outer world. As you forgive, let Love fill you completely. There is not enough hateful energy in the world to ever be larger than Love. This Truth will assure you and you will be centered in Peace.

*Mother Mary, Queen of Peace*

W hat is Peace of mind? It is a practice of mindfulness and letting go. It doesn't last when you think it is related to how much money is in your bank account or how much insurance you have for your life and your things. Practice observing and letting go. Peace of mind, Peace of heart will be yours.

*Jeshua ben Joseph*

*T*hroughout millennia humans have been waiting and hoping for an Era of Peace. It is upon you and you are the cause. Be blessed in your gift of Peace.

*Kalishar, Commander of the Ship of Love*

*D*o you feel at Peace with your neighbors? Do you even know your neighbors? Make Peace with your neighbors. Do not wait for the emergencies of your life to look for them. Expand your awareness. Expand your Love. Expand your Peace.

*Ascended Master Tsen Tsing of the Council*

*T*here is a popular belief among humans that your emotions are what make you feel alive. As long as you hold this above the belief that conscious awareness sustains your connection to Life, however it appears, you will remain addicted to your emotional body's use of your bio-chemicals and hormones. Make Peace with this and feel free.

*Ascended Master Hillarion*

pen your vessel wide that I might pour my Peace in you to overflowing delight.

*Jeshua ben Joseph*

*P*eace will always be available to you when it is your intention. It is the secret prize within everything you see, everything you experience. Make yourself very very still and deepen your breath to a slow and quiet rhythm. There it is. Just beneath your breath. Look for it whenever you are most certain that it is not with you. I assure you, it IS within you.

*Ascended Lady Master Ariana, Goddess of Truth*

*T*here is Peace in darkness and there is Peace in light. There is Peace in activity and there is Peace in stillness. Create your smile to be the natural position of your facial muscles and the world will find Peace in you. The world will smile back which will remind you that you are smiling and in Peace.

*Ascended Lady Master Quan Yin*

*A*llow Peace to enter through all human portals. Do not stop Peace by putting up barriers of "false protection". Bless all that you do not recognize as Peace, for you may be fooled to believe the disguises of the trickster mind are real. Only Love is real. Only Peace is real.

*Cosmic Buddha*

*W*hat is Peace when it is demanded on the papers of war? Perhaps war-like activities may be ordered to cease. That is important for individuals to feel some relief from the constant tension and uncertainty. What is offered to souls to assure ongoing inner Peace when the papers have been signed? What is your personal plan to develop deeper Peace while the outer world makes decisions for you Peace?

*Ascended Master Aswan Dengali*

lease forgive everyone for everything. If you cannot find Peace in every moment, there is more to forgive.

*Ascended Master Tsen Tsing of the Council*

*T*here are no lines between Peace and whatever else there could possibly be which represents "no peace" in your life. Go to your still place within and let yourself feel the "no peace" experience. Now simply think, 'I Am Peace' while you breathe in deeply. Notice what has happened to the "no peace" place in you.

*Ascended Master Djwal Khul*

*L*iving aware of every moment and blessing every moment is a certain path for Peace within. It is a certain path for Ascension.

*Ascended Master Lord Lanto*

*L*et yourself imagine that all the stress of this day is melting, falling from you into pools of clear cool water at your feet. Now imagine that the pools of water merge into a pond that deepens and expands the more you let go and allow your breath to de-stress every thought and emotion. Imagine that the pond lifts you just enough so that you are floating comfortably on the water. If you are not a swimmer, let that stress go and imagine that there are soothing hands holding you up as you relax into the pond. Breathe in Peace. Breathe out Love. Breathe in Peace. Breathe out Love. Have a wonderful meditation . . .

*Ascended Lady Master Ariana,*
*Goddess of Truth*

*T*he Violet Flame of Transmutation is not a gimmick. It is a very real energy and tool that has been given to humanity. Whether you use some popular decrees or simply visualize the Violet Flame and place your limited thoughts, emotions and beliefs into it, you will find that there is a Lightening of your spirit and embodiment. Whatever stands between you and perfect Peace, we now observe it moving through the Violet Flame of Transmutation and issuing forth the Golden White Light of Source.

*Ascended Master Saint Germain*

W hat price Peace? Placing restraints on a person who acts frenetically or violently is a temporary solution to assist in stilling the energy so that Peace may be more available. Bombing a country to still frenetic and warlike conduct is again, only a temporary solution to find Peace. It happens mostly in comic films that hysterical people get slapped in the face to stop their behavior and the response is "Thanks, I needed that." Truly, do you need that? Do you desire that? Bless yourself and your world by breathing deeply and with reverence. Therein is the Peace.

*Ascended Master Batu Khan*
*(grandson of Genghis Khan)*

*W*ill you allow Peace to carry Justice so that all humanity is blessed? The good news is that you do not need to carry Justice on your shoulders. You can trust that Lady Justice rides on the intention of Peace and awakens humanity to the Truth. No screaming. No demanding. Simply be centered in Peace and intend that Justice is doing her job. You do not need to figure it out and keep score. Peace. Namaste.

*Ascended Master Saint Germain*

*T*hank you for the thoughts of Peace that you are bringing forth. The energy of Peace emanating from each of you is becoming more and more radiant. This is important for your personal experience and expression of Divine Creation, and indeed for all within the Whole of Creation. The various ministries of Spirit rejoice that your consciousness is merging with All That Is.

*Ascended Master Sanat Kumara*

*W*hen someone says or does something that seems violent in your "space", and you can carry a smile within and respond only with compassion . . . you will recognize the Peace Mastery you have integrated. Keep practicing Peace and no one and nothing will remove you from your Center. It is possible. While in a meditative state, imagine a situation from your "past" that involved reacting to a violent energy. Now, imagine yourself responding in a state of Peace. Namaste.

*Ascended Lady Master Nada*

W ithin you is a Master Artist seeking to express Beauty, Grace, Peace and Love to the world. If you breathe deeply and smile, you cannot fail your perfect Master expression. Choose the name of your Artful gift to the world. This is called your intention. Thank you, Beloved Ones!

*Archangel Uriel*

*A*nd so . . . life as you know it is constantly changing. With the promise of Peace in every breath, we believe you will enjoy the journey of change and create it to be exuberant transformation. Ask your Soul, "What shall I choose next?" Whatever the answer, we trust that Peace will fill it. Namaste.

*Ascended Master Saint Germain*

*A*re you curious about what is beneath the surface, or over the hill, or around the bend? Do you anticipate the outcome of every thought? Being as a child, explore your life. Be joyful in each moment with glee that in each new moment there is more to experience. Life is full of clues of its synchronicity. Let yourself know Peace that you do not have to script the world. Let yourself know Peace that you get to choose the path.

*Ascended Master Lady Bridgette of Brittany*

*T*his day I AM Peace. I AM Peace now. Continue to affirm this Truth. And So It Is.

*Archangel Michael*

*T*hank you for blessing everyone with Peaceful thoughts. For some, the addiction to adrenaline surges is a barrier to feeling the profound essence of Peace. When you are in Peace and bless others with that energy, you help them be able to bring Peace into their enthusiasm for life. Do you recognize that your can be exuberant and Peaceful at the same time?

*Ascended Master Lord Lanto*

*A*llow all that comes into your path to move through. Please do not block or hinder with your fear, anger or judgment. Be as the full river that runs over its banks with the rains. It allows the water to merge and then it flows where it will. There may be rocks and trees which seem to block the flow, but that does not block. It creates new pathways. There is room for everything to be harmonious and Peaceful.

*Ascended Master Djwal Khul*

*B*eloved Ones, when all is reviewed and your life choices are seen as complete, you will be given the choice to be cleared of the human life and returned to Source, or to return to embodiment and continue to explore. There is Peace in knowing that in the Divine perspective it is all equal and is blessed. My question for you is this ~ will you wait for "death" to be complete? Find your Peace now and be blessed with every choice

*Jeshua ben Joseph*

*T*here is a saying you have in your realms that is, "What goes around comes around." Do you not find Peace in that? There is nothing you have to control. All that is required for your benefit is to be highly conscious of what you speak and what actions you choose. You are not in charge of anyone else's choices. Breathe into that notion and feel the Peace as you let go.

*Ascended Master Tsen Tsing of the Council*

*M*ay Peace fill every heart. May all know everlasting Peace. May all thoughts of anger, fear and blame be transmuted to joy, love and compassion. May Peace guide every soul to its fullest expression and purpose. So Be It! And So It Is!

*Ascended Master Saint Germain*

*H*ave you ever wondered how the Ascended Masters and Angels can continue to hold Peace when your world seems to run amok? It is because we have created our entire Being to be observant and detached from outcomes. You can train yourselves in this process also. Have a breath, laugh and let go.

*Archangel Uriel*

*T*he silence contains the most wondrous sounds of the Universe. If you sit in Peaceful quietude, you will discover how your frequency harmonizes with the frequencies of All That Is

*Ascended Master Kuthumi*

W hen you are at the grocery market, be in Peace. When you are driving in traffic, be in Peace. When you are waiting for service, be in Peace. When you are texting from your phone, be in Peace. When you are preparing a meal, be in Peace. When you are paying your bills, be in Peace. When you are waiting "on hold", be in Peace. When you are explaining to your children that you do not approve of their request, be in Peace. When you open another "pass this on" email, be in Peace. When you discover that your favorite shirt has a stain on it, be in Peace. When you are watching television and your program is interrupted, be in Peace. Of course, we could go on, and on. How many opportunities have you had this day to be in Peace? Maybe you forgot. Choose now to be in Peace.

*Ascended Master Tsen Tsing of the Council*

*I* f you are feeling tangled in the stress of a day's tasks and challenges you deserve to gift yourself with a couple of minutes of letting yourself go. Picture this—a desk telephone coil is tightly wound and twisted. You lift the receiver and while you hold the cord at its connection to the phone, you allow the handset to dangle toward the floor. Watch as it unfurls and loosens the knots while retaining its nature of design. You can sit quietly having several deep cleansing breaths and imagine that the Universe is holding onto your silver cord while you let go and let yourself unwind. You are totally supported and connected to the Source. This is a brief exercise in participating with the Universe as Peace can now flow through the cord without being blocked by your tangled energies.

*Archangel Metatron*

*G*ot Peace?
This message brought to you by the Council of Shambala. Remember to have many, many servings of Peace each day. Your life depends on it.

*Ascended Master Tsen Tsing of the Council*

*O*ne World. One People. One Peace. When one is in a state of unrest, One feels it and sends Love to that place of pain. One Love heals all and One Peace remains.

*Ascended Lady Master Nada*

*W*ithin the world you currently experience, there is a human cry for peace. We can hear a parent crying, "I just want to come home from work and have peace and quiet!" We can hear a neighbor crying, "We need more police to keep the peace around here." We can hear the political leader crying, "I promise peace if you vote for me." We still say, all the Peace you desire is within you and within your world. Shift your response. Breathe deeply and proclaim Peace Now.

*Ascended Lady Master Quan Yin*

*L*ook into the eyes of a well-fed baby and notice how much excitement is carried in the Peace that shines. Look into a mirror and let your soul demonstrate that same look of excitement and Peace. This is a great practice. It will be easier for you to see those qualities in the eyes of everyone so that they can see it in your eyes.

*Chief White Eagle*

I

Am

Peace

# Dawn Katar

Spiritually connected with her Angels since early childhood, Dawn Katar has offered spiritual counseling and teaching for over forty years. She has shared healing messages of hope with people all around the world and has helped many to open their own perfect channel of Divine Light. Dawn Katar has held administrative positions for several organizations in addition to her spiritual work. One of her passions has been raising awareness for children's mental health. She has served as an advocate and supporter of parents raising children with emotional and mental challenges.

Dawn Katar is married to her Twin Flame, Darryl and has two children. The family currently resides in Scottsdale, Arizona. Dawn Katar is currently working on other compilations of her channeled work as well and is writing, along with her husband, a manual for Ascension.

For more about Dawn Katar and her work, go to www.openchannelresources.com